Living the
Divine Mercy

A Pocket Guide to

Living the Divine Mercy

Rev. George W. Kosicki, C.S.B.

Our Sunday Visitor Publishing Division
Our Sunday Visitor, Inc.
Huntington, Indiana 46750

The Scripture citations used in this work are taken from the *Second Catholic Edition of the Revised Standard Version of the Bible* (RSV), copyright © 1965, 1966, and 2006 by the Division of Christian Education of the National Council of the Churches of Christ in the United States of America. Used by permission. All rights reserved.

English translations of papal and other Vatican documents are from the Vatican website, www.vatican.va.

Quotations from *Diary: St. Maria Faustina Kowalska: Divine Mercy in My Soul* copyright © 1987 by the Congregation of Marians of the Immaculate Conception, Stockbridge, MA 01263. All rights reserved. Used with permission.

Every reasonable effort has been made to determine copyright holders of excerpted materials and to secure permissions as needed. If any copyrighted materials have been inadvertently used in this work without proper credit being given in one form or another, please notify Our Sunday Visitor in writing so that future printings of this work may be corrected accordingly.

Copyright © 2008 by Our Sunday Visitor Publishing Division,
Our Sunday Visitor, Inc. Published 2008

13 12 11 10 09 08   1 2 3 4 5 6 7 8 9

All rights reserved. With the exception of short excerpts for critical reviews, no part of this work may be reproduced or transmitted in any form or by any means whatsoever without permission in writing from the publisher. Write:

Our Sunday Visitor Publishing Division
Our Sunday Visitor, Inc.
200 Noll Plaza
Huntington, IN 46750

ISBN: 978-1-59276-279-8 (Inventory No. T368)

LCCN: 2007940659

Cover design by Amanda Miller
Interior design by Sherri L. Hoffman

Divine Mercy Image copyright © Congregation of Marians of the Immaculate Conception, Stockbridge, MA 01263, www.marian.org. Used with permission.

PRINTED IN THE UNITED STATES OF AMERICA

Table of Contents

Introduction   7

1. What Is Life All About?   13
2. Jesus Is the Way to the Father's House   17
3. Each Saint Followed Jesus as the Way to the Father's House   21
4. The Merciful Way of St. Faustina   29
5. How We, Too, Can Be Saints   49
6. Pope John Paul II's Ways of Living the Divine Mercy   53
7. Practical Ways to Live the Merciful Way   59

Introduction

Now that Sister Faustina Kowalska of the Most Blessed Sacrament has been canonized by Pope John Paul II, she is enrolled in the major leagues of saints. By her canonization, on the Second Sunday of Easter, April 30, 2000, John Paul II declared her a *model* for us to follow in our spiritual pilgrimage and a unique and special *member* of the Body of Christ, now interceding for the Church and the whole world for God's mercy.

In addition, when John Paul II declared that "the Second Sunday of Easter ... from now on throughout the Church *will be called 'Divine Mercy Sunday'*" (April 30, 2000, n. 4), he also "canonized" the Divine Mercy message and devotion, since Divine Mercy Sunday is the main revelation of Our Lord to St. Faustina, and which capsulizes all of the Divine Mercy message and devotion.

In yet another declaration, the Holy Father declared that the message of Divine Mercy is *the message* for the third millennium, to all people, as "God's gift to our time." He repeated this strong affirmation of "a gift of God for our time" three times, assuring us that the light of mercy gives us hope and comfort, as we abandon ourselves in trust, in the midst of the suffering of our time.

John Paul exhorted us to sing with St. Faustina, whose "life was a hymn of mercy," and with "Mary, Mother of Divine Mercy, the first soloist of the choir of heaven and earth" (farewell ceremony at Fátima, May 13, 1982): "I will sing of your mercies, O LORD, for ever" (Ps 89:1).

In the light of this twofold "canonization," and of the condition of the world, Pope John Paul II expressed a strong *urgency* about turning to God's mercy now, while there is still time for mercy:

- "Where, if not in the Divine Mercy, can the world find refuge and the light of hope?" (beatification of Sister Faustina, April 18, 1993).

- "There is nothing that mankind needs more than Divine Mercy" (at the Shrine of Divine Mercy in Poland, June 7, 1997).
- "Mankind will not have peace until it turns with trust to My mercy" (*Diary: St. Maria Faustina Kowalska: Divine Mercy in My Soul* [hereafter *Diary*], 300, which records the words of Our Lord, quoted by the Pope in his homily at the canonization of St. Faustina)

In his homily at the Mass of Canonization, Pope John Paul II expressed the need to *welcome* mercy, to welcome Jesus, to receive Him, and to *experience* His mercy by trusting Him and so be enabled to be merciful, even as our heavenly Father is merciful (see Lk 6:36).

On what would eventually be recognized as Divine Mercy Sunday, John Paul II, in 1994, exhorted us to *experience* the mercy of God:

> As people of this restless time of ours, wavering between the emptiness of self-exaltation and the humiliation of despair, *we have a greater need than ever for a regenerating experience of mercy.* (*Regina Caeli* talk [April 10, 1994], emphasis in original)

And again, in 1995, the Pope said:

> We must personally experience this mercy, if, in turn, we want to be capable of mercy. *Let us learn to forgive!* The spiral of hatred and violence which stains with blood the path of so many individuals and nations can only be broken by the *miracle of forgiveness*. (*Regina Caeli* talk [April 23, 1995], emphasis in original)

This need to *experience* God's mercy is expressed by Our Lord and recorded by St. Faustina. Our Lord expresses this need in a two-fold desire:

> *I desire* **that the whole world know My infinite mercy.** *I desire* **to grant unimaginable graces to those souls who trust in My mercy.** (*Diary*, 687 [all words of Our Lord are in bold type], emphasis added)

But there are so many voices, so many calls, so many ways! Which way is for you and me? There are so many saints to imitate! But we often complain: "So many of them are beyond my capability! I am so inadequate, weak, and miserable!"

Thanks be to God, there is a way for the inadequate, the weak, and the miserable! It is *the merciful way* that St. Faustina proclaimed from the beginning to the very end of her *Diary*. It is, as John Paul II said, the message and the way for the third millennium.

Consider a few fascinating "statistics" about St. Faustina's *Diary* as a promise of hope for you and me:

- Some 120 times, she speaks of her own misery, and ours.
- But some 240 times — twice as many as "misery" — she speaks of her *trust* in the Lord.
- But even more encouraging, she speaks of God's *mercy* some 1,200 times — ten times more about misery!

This is the purpose of the merciful way: to let you know and to convince you that God's mercy is infinite. God's mercy is greater than all the misery and sin of the world combined — especially your sin and misery!

Now is the time to turn to His mercy with trust and to "find comfort in all [our] anxieties and fears" (Pope John Paul II, at the Shrine of Divine Mercy in Poland, June 7, 1997). In this little book, it is my hope that you will find the way of living the Divine Mercy of Our Lord as He taught it to St. Faustina.

Jesus, I trust in You!

Chapter 1

What Is Life All About?

What is life on earth all about? It is about eternal life!

We are made by God to know Him, to love Him, and to serve Him in this life, and to be happy with Him forever in the next. We are created by God to be part of His great plan of eternal life. His plan is to have a great family that shares in His love and life.

But our first parents failed the test. They rebelled against God by an act of disobedience. They lost their holy innocence. They lost their way to eternal life, and death entered the world (see Gen 3).

Fortunately, God promised a redeemer to bring us the gift of eternal life. God so loved the world and mankind, which He had created, that He gave His only Son, Jesus Christ, in atonement for our sins and the sin of our first parents, so that whoever would *trust in Him* would not die but have eternal life (see Jn 3:16).

And there is the rub! *Trusting in Him.* Trusting in Jesus Christ is a free act of the will, a believing faith in Him. It "means 'to abandon oneself' to the truth of the word of the living God" (Pope John Paul II, *Mother of the Redeemer* [1987], n. 14).

To trust is a decision, an act of our free will. It is this free-will act that God asks for, expects, and waits for. He created us with a free will and intelligence, and He will not violate that freedom which He created. And so, He waits for our act of trust, our "yes" to His plan, in order to flood us with His love and eternal life.

Our T.R.U.S.T. is a:

Total
Reliance
Upon
Saving
Truth — Jesus Christ!

What we receive by trust in Jesus is a new life, eternal life in Christ, which is a gift of His love poured into our hearts (see Rom 5:5), which we call *mercy*. This M.E.R.C.Y. is the gift of God Himself, who is "**Love and Mercy itself**" (*Diary*, 1074):

Mighty
Eternal
Redeeming
Compassionate
Yahweh

The first act of God's mercy is to forgive our sins. As we receive God's mercy and have our sins forgiven, we in turn are to be merciful to others and forgive them. Our redemption is the forgiveness of sins (see Col 1:14).

As we receive God's loving mercy in Christ Jesus, we enter into God's plan for our life; we enter into eternal life as members of the family of God.

Chapter 2

Jesus Is the Way to the Father's House

On the night before Jesus died, during His Last Supper discourse, He told His disciples the Way:

> "Let not your hearts be troubled; believe in God, believe also in me. In my Father's house are many rooms; if it were not so, would I have told you that I go to prepare a place for you? And when I go and prepare a place for you, I will come again and will take you to myself, that where I am you may be also. And you know the way where I am going." Thomas said to him, "Lord, we do not know where you are going; how can we know the way?" Jesus said to him, "*I am the way*, and the truth, and the life; no one comes to the Father, but by me. (Jn 14:1-6, emphasis added)

Jesus Himself is the way to the Father's house! Jesus doesn't draw a map to show us the way.

Rather, He points to Himself as *the Way*. This means we must be united with Jesus, one with Him by our *trust*, which is our "faithing," hoping, and loving Him that makes us united with Him as He takes us on the pilgrimage to the Father's house.

This is Good News! This is the Gospel.

The Gospel in one word is *Jesus*. And in three words the Gospel is: *Jesus Christ (is) Lord!*

The three words give His name — Jesus — with the two titles of Christ and Lord, which are the primitive creed that summarizes the life and mission of Jesus. The three words can be presented in a table that capsulizes the mission of Jesus and our response as His disciples:

GOSPEL:	JESUS	CHRIST (IS)	LORD
Scripture:	died	rose	reigns
Disciples:	die to self	rise with Him	reign with Him
Sacraments:	Baptism	Confirmation	Eucharist
By trust:	faith	hope	love
As we:	repent	yield	abide
In steps/stages:	purgative	illuminative	unitive

The three dimensions of the Gospel of *Jesus Christ (is) Lord* are like three steps in a dance with the Lord. As in a dance, the three steps are repeated over and over again. We die, rise, and reign with Him as we repent, yield, and abide in Him, whirling in higher and higher spirals with the Lord, ever closer in union with Him, all the *way* to the Father's house!

Chapter 3

Each Saint Followed Jesus as the Way to the Father's House

All of the saints officially recognized by the Church followed *Jesus* as the Way, the Truth, and the Life (see Jn 14:6). They followed as His disciples by their daily *dying* to self and sin, *rising* with Him by the Holy Spirit, and *reigning* with Him in His Father's kingdom. They lived a life of trust: a life of faith, of hope, and of love. The pattern of all of the holy disciples of Jesus followed the traditional way of purgation, illumination, and union described by Origen, an early Church Father, as stages of the mystical ascent to God.

But all of the saints expressed their pilgrimage with the Lord in unique and precious ways, as gems in the great mosaic of God's family. Each had to climb the mountain of the Lord along the path the Lord chose for them.

Consider the unique ways that the following saints followed Jesus as the Way.

St. John of the Cross

This Doctor of the Church, who was also one of the greatest mystics, followed and taught *the dark way*: dark because God acts and speaks in darkness and silence; dark because we walk in the darkness of faith; dark because there is so much light from God that we cannot see. When a person follows St. John's teaching and example, the Lord Jesus, the Bridegroom, is able to purify and prepare His pilgrim bride for total surrender to Himself in love.

St. Thérèse of Lisieux

This spiritual daughter of St. John of the Cross and Doctor of the Church, learned of St. John of the Cross through her community teaching and the little book of his *Maxims*. She held on to her little book of maxims, and read and re-read them (see *John and Thérèse: Flames of Love: The Influence of St. John of the Cross in the Life and Writings of St. Thérèse of Lisieux*, Bishop Guy Gaucher [Alba House, 1999], p. 65).

Like St. John of the Cross, Thérèse lived a life of faith, hope, and love, but developed, followed, and taught *the Little Way*. Her Little Way is the way of love. Her vocation was to be love in the heart of the Church, inspired by St. Paul's canticle of love (see 1 Cor 12:31 and 1 Cor 13). "But earnestly desire the higher gifts. And I will show you a still more excellent way" (1 Cor 12:31) — the way of love — the Little Way. We, too, are called to be love in the heart of the Church; to go to the Father as a little child, being lifted up by Him into His loving arms.

St. Ignatius of Loyola

This founder of the Jesuits and great teacher of the spiritual life lived and taught his followers *the discerning way*. His work *Spiritual Exercises* is a basic training course in discerning our mission in a life based on the Gospels. He taught how to discern God's will, and then how to follow it wholeheartedly to the glory of God the Father. His discerning way is incarnational, stressing both the divinity and the humanity of Christ. He developed practical ways of knowing God's will for his followers.

St. Margaret Mary Alacoque

The "apostle of the Sacred Heart of Jesus" lived a life of faith, hope, and love in the convent of

Paray-le-Monial, France. Our Lord appeared to her in visions of the Sacred Heart, giving her a mission to the Church. She was called to a special response from herself and from the Church: a response of reparation and consolation to the Sacred Heart of Jesus, who is so deeply in love with mankind and yet is mostly ignored by ingratitude and irreverence. She knew the suffering and pain of the Heart of Jesus, and she responded with love in what I would call *the heartfelt way*.

St. Faustina
This humble Polish nun built on the example and teachings of the great saints who had gone before her.

Like St. John of the Cross, she went through the dark nights of the soul, and her spirit reached the summit of mystical union with her spouse, Jesus Christ. She had only *one* desire: to be a great saint and to glorify God's mercy. She integrated into her life the teachings of St. John's *Ascent of Mount Carmel*, the *Dark Night*, the *Spiritual Canticle*, and the *Living Flame of Love* by her *trust*. Her trust was a total abandonment to the truth of

God's word; it was living faith, hope, and love in action. Like St. John of the Cross, she was a master of trust. Yet, in a unique and precious way of complete trust in God's mercy in the midst of our misery, she developed *the merciful way*.

Like St. Thérèse of Lisieux, St. Faustina lived *the Little Way* by pure love of God (see *Diary*, 570 and 778). She, too, trusted in the merciful love (see *Diary*, 1489). She, too, had bold desires: to love God like no one ever loved before (see *Diary*, 267); to be a priest, missionary, preacher, and martyr (see *Diary*, 302). She, too, offered herself as a victim of merciful love for the salvation of souls (see *Diary*, 135-138).

Like St. Ignatius of Loyola, she considered God's will as "Love and Mercy itself" (see, for example, *Diary*, 1264 and 1574); under the direction of the Lord, on a blank sheet of paper, she made a big "X" as a sign of crossing out her own will. From then on, it would be only God's will. It was her determination to "do the Will of God everywhere, always, and in everything" (*Diary*, 374). Further, St. Faustina was trained in the spiritual life by Father Joseph Andrasz, a Jesuit who was her confessor in Kraków, Poland,

and who helped the young religious to discern her call and led her in making the Ignatian spiritual exercises (see *Spiritual Exercises*, annotation 19).

Like St. Margaret Mary, St. Faustina had a great love of the Sacred and Merciful Heart of Jesus. The focus of the Sacred Heart message and devotion is on reparation and consolation; its prime direction is within. The focus of the Merciful Heart of Jesus is on receiving mercy in order to be merciful; its prime direction is without. In a sense, St. Faustina's devotion to the Merciful Heart is a summary of the Divine Mercy message and devotion because the Heart of Jesus is so prominent in each of the devotions Our Lord taught St. Faustina. It is a "new impetus" given to the devotion of the Sacred Heart (see *Heart of the Redeemer*, Timothy O'Donnell [Ignatius Press, 1992], p. 239). And like St. Margaret Mary, St. Faustina had visions and revelations from Our Lord that were for the whole Church and the world.

Now the "great apostle of the Divine Mercy for our time" — as John Paul II called St. Faustina — has taken her own place with St. John of the Cross, St. Thérèse of Lisieux, St.

Ignatius of Loyola, St. Margaret Mary Alacoque, and many others as a member of what I call the "Dream Team" of great saints in heaven!

What is so special about the merciful way of St. Faustina? This is what we have to explore and explain in the following chapters.

Chapter 4
The Merciful Way of St. Faustina

Like the great saints before her, St. Faustina lived and taught us a unique way of following *the Way*, Jesus Christ, in our pilgrimage to the Father's house. In her life, she blended the life and teachings of the great saints and yet expressed her spiritual life in a way that can be lived by the ordinary person and by persons who feel inadequate and unable to follow the great saints. Her merciful way opens up the way to holiness for everyone, especially poor sinners and the miserable. At the same time, the merciful way is the way for those seeking perfection on the way with the Lord.

Let us look at the various ways St. Faustina described the merciful way in her *Diary*.

1. In Your Misery, Plunge Into the Ocean of God's Mercy With Complete Trust

Some 120 times, St. Faustina writes of misery, describing her own misery, and how she plunges and immerses herself into the infinite ocean of Divine Mercy with great trust. From the early entries of her *Diary* through the end of her life, she records her awareness of the abyss of her misery that is filled by the abyss of God's mercy. For example:

> Thank You, Jesus, for the great favor of making known to me the whole abyss of my misery. I know that I am an abyss of nothingness and that, if Your holy grace did not hold me up, I would return to nothingness in a moment. And so, with every beat of my heart, I thank You, my God, for Your great mercy towards me. (*Diary*, 256)
>
> Holy Trinity, One God, incomprehensible in the greatness of Your mercy for creatures, and especially for poor sinners, You have made known the abyss of Your mercy, incomprehensible and unfathomable [as it is] to any mind, whether of man or angel. Our nothingness and our misery are drowned in Your greatness. O infinite goodness, who can ever praise You sufficiently? Can there be found a soul that understands You in Your love? O Jesus, there are such souls, but they are few. (*Diary*, 361)

St. Faustina knew she lived for the benefit of many souls:

📖 I know that I live, not for myself, but for a great number of souls. I know that graces granted me are not for me alone, but for souls. O Jesus, the abyss of Your mercy has been poured into my soul, which is an abyss of misery itself. Thank You, Jesus, for the graces and the pieces of the Cross which You give me at each moment of my life. (*Diary*, 382)

St. Faustina shares with us her way of responding to tribulation:

📖 Amid the greatest torments, I fix the gaze of my soul upon Jesus Crucified; I do not expect help from people, but place my trust in God. In His unfathomable mercy lies all my hope. (*Diary*, 681)

She desired to prepare the world — especially the miserable — for the coming of the Lord:

📖 I am reliving these moments with Our Lady. With great longing, I am waiting for the Lord's coming. Great are my desires. I desire that all humankind come to know the Lord. I would like to prepare all nations for the coming of the Word Incarnate. O Jesus, make the fount of Your mercy gush forth more abundantly, for humankind is seriously ill and thus has more need than ever of Your compassion. You are a bottomless sea of mercy for us sinners; and the greater the misery, the more right we have to Your mercy. You are a fount which makes all creatures happy by Your infinite mercy. (*Diary*, 793)

St. Faustina was concerned about the last hour of dying persons:

> All grace flows from mercy, and the last hour abounds with mercy for us. Let no one doubt concerning the goodness of God; even if a person's sins were as dark as night, God's mercy is stronger than our misery. One thing alone is necessary: that the sinner set ajar the door of his heart, be it ever so little, to let in a ray of God's merciful grace, and then God will do the rest. But poor is the soul who has shut the door on God's mercy, even at the last hour. It

was just such souls who plunged Jesus into deadly sorrow in the Garden of Olives; indeed, it was from His Most Merciful Heart that divine mercy flowed out. (*Diary*, 1507)

She records the words of Our Lord about distressed souls:

> Write this for the benefit of distressed souls; when a soul sees and realizes the gravity of its sins, when the whole abyss of the misery into which it immersed itself is displayed before its eyes, let it not despair, but with trust let it throw itself into the arms of My mercy, as a child into the arms of its beloved mother. These souls have a right of priority to My compassionate Heart, they have first access to My mercy. Tell them that no soul that has called upon My mercy has been disappointed or brought to shame. I delight particularly in a soul which has placed its trust in My goodness.
>
> Write that when they say this chaplet in the presence of the dying, I will stand between My Father and the dying person,

not as the just Judge but as the merciful Savior. (*Diary*, 1541)

Of the many entries on trusting in God's mercy, the most powerful entry for me is the one in which the Lord confronts St. Faustina:

> O my Jesus, in thanksgiving for Your many graces, I offer You my body and soul, intellect and will, and all the sentiments of my heart. Through the vows, I have given myself entirely to You; I have then nothing more that I can offer You. Jesus said to me, **My daughter, you have not offered Me that which is really yours.** I probed deeply into myself and found that I love God with all the faculties of my soul and, unable to see what it was that I had not yet given to the Lord, I asked, "Jesus, tell me what it is, and I will give it to You at once with a generous heart." Jesus said to me with kindness, **Daughter, give Me your misery, because it is your exclusive property.** At that moment, a ray of light illumined my soul, and I saw the whole abyss of my misery. In that same moment I nestled close to the Most Sacred

Heart of Jesus with so much trust that even if I had the sins of all the damned weighing on my conscience, I would not have doubted God's mercy but, with a heart crushed to dust, I would have thrown myself into the abyss of Your mercy. I believe, O Jesus, that You would not reject me, but would absolve me through the hand of Your representative. (*Diary*, 1318)

"... Even if I had the sins of all the damned weighing on my conscience!" What a picture of misery! But with total trust in Jesus, she writes: "I would have thrown myself into the abyss of Your mercy."

At the end of her *Diary*, she writes how she followed the merciful way:

> One day during Holy Mass, the Lord gave me a deeper knowledge of His holiness and His majesty, and at the same time I saw my own misery. This knowledge made me happy, and my soul drowned itself completely in His mercy. I felt enormously happy. (*Diary*, 1801)

And in her last entry in the *Diary*, she again expresses how she lived the merciful way:

> One day, when I was preparing for Holy Communion and noticed that I had nothing to offer Him, I fell at His feet, calling down all His mercy upon my poor soul: "May Your grace, which flows down upon me from Your Compassionate Heart, strengthen me for the struggle and sufferings, that I may remain faithful to You. And, although I am such misery, I do not fear You, because I know Your mercy well. Nothing will frighten me away from You, O God, because everything is so much less than what I know [Your mercy to be] — I see that clearly. (*Diary*, 1803)

Through her *Diary*, St. Faustina taught us to trust the mercy of God no matter how miserable or sinful we are. This is her mission now, in heaven, among the great saints:

> I feel certain that my mission will not come to an end upon my death, but will begin. O doubting souls, I will draw aside for you the veils of heaven to convince you

of God's goodness, so that you will no longer continue to wound with your distrust the sweetest Heart of Jesus. God is Love and Mercy. (*Diary*, 281)

The merciful way of St. Faustina is the way of mercy in action. Our Lord made it very clear to her that we must be merciful to others for the love of Him:

> My daughter, if I demand through you that people revere My mercy, you should be the first to distinguish yourself by this confidence in My mercy. I demand from you deeds of mercy, which are to arise out of love for Me. You are to show mercy to your neighbors always and everywhere. You must not shrink from this or try to excuse or absolve yourself from it.
>
> I am giving you three ways of exercising mercy toward your neighbor: the first — by deed, the second — by word, the third — by prayer. In these three degrees is contained the fullness of mercy, and it is an unquestionable proof of love for Me. By this means a soul glorifies and pays reverence to My mercy. Yes, the first

> Sunday after Easter is the Feast of Mercy, but there must also be acts of mercy, and I demand the worship of My mercy through the solemn celebration of the Feast and through the veneration of the image which is painted. By means of this image I shall grant many graces to souls. It is to be a reminder of the demands of My mercy, because even the strongest faith is of no avail without works. O my Jesus, You yourself must help me in everything, because You see how very little I am, and so I depend solely on Your goodness, O God. (*Diary*, 742)

"Blessed are the merciful, for they shall obtain mercy" (Mt 5:7).

"Be merciful, even as your Father is merciful" (Lk 6:36).

2. Live by Trust in Jesus

Another way St. Faustina lived and taught the merciful way was by trust in Jesus. The signature on the Image of the Merciful Savior is a summary of the Divine Mercy message and devotion:

Jesus, I trust in You!

Jesus, who is love and mercy itself (see *Diary*, 1074), is always loving and always merciful. To be merciful is God's part. But He waits for our free welcome and acceptance of His gift of merciful love by our trust in Him. Trust is an act of our free will that expresses faith (belief), hope, and love. Pope John Paul II described what it means to believe, or to trust: "To believe [trust] means 'to abandon oneself' to the truth of the word of the living God, knowing 'how unsearchable are his judgments and how inscrutable his ways' (Rom 11:33)" (*Mother of the Redeemer* [1987], n. 14).

Trust is our part in the covenant that establishes our relationship with God as members of His family (see T.R.U.S.T. on page 14).

Trust in God is one of the great ways to express our love for God. Distrust of God, on the other hand, is one of the great pains Jesus complains about to St. Faustina (see, for example, *Diary*, 50 and 300).

Our Lord's words to St. Faustina about her trust are a great encouragement to us:

> After Holy Communion, I heard these words: — **You see what you are of yourself, but do not be frightened at this. If I**

were to reveal to you the whole misery that you are, you would die of terror. However, be aware of what you are. Because you are such great misery, I have revealed to you the whole ocean of My mercy. I seek and desire souls like yours, but they are few. Your great trust in Me forces Me to continuously grant you graces. You have great and incomprehensible rights over My Heart, for you are a daughter of complete trust. You would not have been able to bear the magnitude of the love which I have for you if I had revealed it to you fully here on earth. I often give you a glimpse of it, but know that this is only an exceptional grace from Me. My love and mercy knows no bounds.** (*Diary*, 718)

The graces of trust are especially a great encouragement to poor sinners:

Today, I heard these words: **The graces I grant you are not for you alone, but for a great number of other souls as well.... And your heart is My constant dwelling place, despite the misery that you are. I unite Myself with you, take away your misery**

> and give you My mercy. I perform works of mercy in every soul. The greater the sinner, the greater the right he has to My mercy. My mercy is confirmed in every work of My hands. He who trusts in My mercy will not perish, for all his affairs are Mine, and his enemies will be shattered at the base of My footstool. (*Diary*, 723)

Some 240 times St. Faustina speaks of trust and records the words of Our Lord. The book *Revelations of Divine Mercy: Daily Readings from the Diary of St. Faustina* (compiled by George W. Kosicki, C.S.B. [Servant Publications, 1996 (now a division of St. Anthony Messenger Press]) dedicates the month of April to readings on trust.

The wonderful *Diary* of St. Faustina records some 1,200 entries on God's mercy, a mercy that is greater than all the misery of the world, and which waits for our trust. The very repetition of the prayer "Jesus, I trust in You!" expresses our trust — and *is* in fact trusting in Jesus.

3. Live Immersed in God's Mercy

Many times St. Faustina records for us the Lord's instructions to immerse herself and others in His ocean of mercy. She uses the terms "plunge," "drown," "transformed into mercy" — all of which could also be described by the Greek word *baptizmo* ("to immerse," to baptize). To be baptized in His mercy is to be transformed into His mercy.

St. Faustina prayed: "I want to be completely transformed into Your mercy.... O my Jesus, transform me into Yourself, for you can do all things" (*Diary*, 163).

Our Lord told her to immerse various groups of people in the novena to the Divine Mercy: **"On each day you will bring to My Heart a different group of souls, and you will immerse them in this ocean of My Mercy...."** (*Diary*, 1209).

Repeatedly, St. Faustina expressed her immersion in God's mercy, plunging into the ocean of His mercy, drowning in mercy with trust:

> Today the Lord's gaze shot through me suddenly, like lightning. At once, I came to know the tiniest specks in my soul, and knowing the depths of my misery, I fell to my knees and begged the Lord's pardon, *and with great trust I immersed myself in His infinite mercy.* Such knowledge does

not depress me nor keep me away from the Lord, but rather it arouses in my soul greater love and boundless trust. The repentance of my heart is linked to love. These extraordinary flashes from the Lord educate my soul. O sweet rays of God, enlighten me to the most secret depth, for I want to arrive at the greatest possible purity of heart and soul. (*Diary*, 852, emphasis added)

Love is flooding my soul; *I am plunged into an ocean of love.* I feel that I am swooning and becoming completely lost in Him. (*Diary*, 513, emphasis added)

Part Three of the book *Trust and Mercy: The Heart of the Good News* (Rev. George W. Kosicki [Franciscan University Press, 1993], pp. 69-112) develops living *baptized in His mercy*. There are many practical suggestions on how to "live baptized in His mercy." I would like to gather these suggested ways to trust and to live baptized in the Lord's mercy under three special works of the Holy Spirit — mercy, Mary, and Eucharist:

- *Radiate His mercy* by trust (see *Diary*, 1074).

- *Sing Mary's Magnificat* with your life by glorifying His mercy (see Pope John Paul II, *Rich in Mercy* [1980], nn. 9 and 10; also see *Diary*, 1242).
- *Be living Eucharist* (see *Diary*, 483): be holy, be humble, be merciful (the spiritual characteristics of St. Faustina).

4. "Tell Aching Mankind to Snuggle Close to My Merciful Heart" (*Diary*, 1074)

St. Faustina knew that the Sacred Heart of Jesus was mercy itself. She would take refuge and hide in His Heart. In her experience of her misery, she would *nestle close to the merciful Heart of Jesus* (see *Diary*, 1318) and rest on His Heart (see, for example, *Diary*, 801, 929, and 1348).

Our Lord told her that we, too, should do the same, and that He would fill us with peace:

> Tell [all people], My daughter, that I am Love and Mercy itself. When a soul approaches Me with trust, I fill it with such an abundance of graces that it cannot contain them within itself, but radiates them to other souls. (*Diary*, 1074)

5. The "Perfect Way": Give Glory to God's Mercy

To my great delight, I discovered a passage in St. Faustina's *Diary* that describes her discovery of "a way to give perfect glory" to the mercy of God. It is the only time that she uses the word "way," which gives an insight into her way of mercy. She describes the praise that the saints and angels in heaven give the mercy of God — and then she states that she, too, has found "a way to give perfect glory...."

> Let Your mercy resound throughout the orb of the earth, and let it rise to the foot of Your throne, giving praise to the greatest of Your attributes; that is, Your incomprehensible mercy. O God, this unfathomable mercy enthralls anew all the holy souls and all the spirits of heaven. These pure spirits are immersed in holy amazement as they glorify this inconceivable mercy of God, which in turn arouses even greater admiration in them, and their praise is carried out in a perfect manner. O eternal God, how ardently I desire to glorify this greatest of

Your attributes; namely, Your unfathomable mercy. I see all my littleness, and cannot compare myself to the heavenly beings who praise the Lord's mercy with holy admiration. But I, too, have found a way to give perfect glory to the incomprehensible mercy of God. (*Diary*, 835)

Then, in a dramatic way, St. Faustina builds up to her discovery of *the perfect way* in the final sentence of the next entry in her *Diary*:

O most sweet Jesus, who have deigned to allow miserable me to gain a knowledge of Your unfathomable mercy; O most sweet Jesus, who have graciously demanded that I tell the whole world of Your incomprehensible mercy, this day I take into my hands the two rays that spring from Your merciful Heart; that is, the Blood and the Water; and I scatter them all over the globe so that each soul may receive Your mercy and, having received it, may glorify it for endless ages. O most sweet Jesus who, in Your incomprehensible kindness, have deigned to unite my wretched heart to Your most merciful Heart, *it is with Your own Heart that I glorify God, our Father, as no soul has ever glorified Him before.* (*Diary*, 836, emphasis added)

What a gem! St. Faustina sounds like St. Therésè of Lisieux in her boldness. Here is her great discovery — in union with the merciful Heart of Jesus she gives *perfect glory to the mercy of God the Father!* In this way, she can cover the whole globe with the mercy that springs from the pierced Heart of Jesus!

This is St. Faustina's merciful way!

Later, in her *Diary*, St. Faustina writes of the exclusive task of her life as glorifying God's mercy, reflecting the Heart of Jesus:

> My Jesus, penetrate me through and through so that I might be able to reflect You in my whole life. Divinize me so that my deeds may have supernatural value. Grant that I may have love, compassion and mercy for every soul without exception. O my Jesus, each of Your saints reflects one of Your virtues; I desire to reflect Your compassionate heart, full of mercy; I want to glorify it. Let Your mercy, O Jesus, be impressed upon my heart and

soul like a seal, and this will be my badge in this and the future life. *Glorifying Your mercy is the exclusive task of my life.* (*Diary*, 1242, emphasis added)

How beautifully St. Faustina describes her unique spirituality: "I desire to reflect Your compassionate Heart, full of mercy; I want to glorify it."

Chapter 5

How We, Too, Can Be Saints

St. Faustina had a great desire to be a *great* saint, not just an ordinary saint:

> My Jesus, You know that from my earliest years I have wanted to become a great saint; that is to say, I have wanted to love You with a love so great that there would be no soul who has hitherto loved You so. At first these desires of mine were kept secret, and only Jesus knew of them. But today I cannot contain them within my heart; I would like to cry out to the whole world, "Love God, because He is good and great is His mercy!" (*Diary*, 1372)

And she wanted to be a saint for the welfare of the Church and the benefit of souls:

> I strive for the greatest perfection possible in order to be useful to the Church. Greater by far is my bond to the Church. The sanctity or the fall of each individual

soul has an effect upon the whole Church. Observing myself and those who are close to me, I have come to understand how great an influence I have on other souls, not by any heroic deeds, as these are striking in themselves, but by small actions like a movement of the hand, a look, and many other things too numerous to mention, which have an effect on and reflect in the souls of others, as I myself have noticed. (*Diary*, 1475)

And she taught that we, too, can be saints by a bit of goodwill and faithfulness to the inspirations of the Holy Spirit:

On a certain occasion, I saw a person about to commit a mortal sin. I asked the Lord to send me the greatest torments so that that soul could be saved. Then I suddenly felt the terrible pain of a crown of thorns on my head. It lasted for quite a long time, but that person remained in the Lord's grace. O my Jesus, how very easy it is to become holy; all that is needed is a bit of good will. If Jesus sees this little bit of good will in the soul, He hurries to give himself to the soul, and nothing can stop Him, neither shortcomings nor falls — absolutely nothing. Jesus is anxious to help that soul, and if it is faithful to this grace from God, it can very soon attain the highest holiness possible for a creature here on earth. God is very generous and does not deny His grace to anyone. Indeed He gives more than what we ask of Him. *Faithfulness to the inspirations of the Holy Spirit — that is the shortest route.* (*Diary*, 291, emphasis added)

And she recorded the words of Our Lord that it is His desire that we be saints — and we can be saints *if only we trust in His mercy*, if only we live the merciful way:

> Today, in the course of a long conversation, the Lord said to me, **How very much I desire the salvation of souls! My dearest secretary, write that I want to pour out My divine life into human souls and to sanctify them, if only they were willing to accept My grace.** *The greatest sinners would achieve great sanctity, if only they would trust in My mercy.* **The very inner**

depths of My being are filled to overflowing with mercy, and it is being poured out upon all I have created. My delight is to act in a human soul and to fill it with My mercy and to justify it. My kingdom on earth is My life in the human soul. Write, My secretary, that I Myself am the spiritual guide of souls — and I guide them indirectly through the priest, and lead each one to sanctity by a road known to Me alone. (*Diary*, 1784)

In her teaching on the call to holiness, St. Faustina expressed one of the great themes of the Second Vatican Council and of Pope John Paul II.

Chapter 6
Pope John Paul II's Ways of Living the Divine Mercy

Pope John Paul II also described the merciful way of living the Divine Mercy message and devotion. In his address at the Shrine of Divine Mercy in Lagiewniki, Kraków, Poland, he described the meaning and power of trusting in Jesus:

> It is a *message that is clear and understandable for everyone.* Anyone can come here, look at this picture of the Merciful Jesus, his Heart radiating grace, and hear in the depths of his own soul what Blessed Faustina heard: *"Fear nothing. I am with you always"* (*Diary*, [586]).
>
> And if this person responds with a sincere heart: *"Jesus, I trust in you!"* he will find comfort in all his *anxieties and fears.* In this dialogue of abandonment, there is established between man and Christ a *special bond that sets love free.* And "there is no fear in love, but

53

perfect love casts out fear" (1 Jn 4:18). (June 7, 1997, emphasis added)

Then he addressed the sisters of the community of St. Faustina, exhorting them to practice, proclaim, and plead mercy for a world in need of mercy:

> Dear Sisters! An extraordinary vocation is yours. Choosing from among you, Blessed Faustina, Christ has made your Congregation the guardian of this place, and at the same time he has called you to a particular apostolate, that of his mercy. I ask you: accept this responsibility!
>
> The people of today need your *proclamation of mercy:* they need your *works of mercy* and they need your *prayer to obtain mercy* [cf. *Diary*, 742]. Do not neglect any of these dimensions of the apostolate. (Emphasis added)

John Paul II also prayed to the Blessed Mother in 1994 that we might live the merciful way:

> O Mary, Mother of mercy! You know the Heart of your divine Son better than anyone. Instill in us the filial trust in Jesus practiced by

the saints, the trust that animated Blessed Faustina Kowalska, the great apostle of Divine Mercy in our time. (Divine Mercy Sunday, April 10, 1994)

And again in 1995:

May Mary obtain this gift of Divine Mercy for all humanity so that the individuals and peoples who are particularly tormented by hostility and fratricidal war may overcome hatred and build concrete attitudes of reconciliation and peace. (Divine Mercy Sunday, April 23, 1995)

Then, at the canonization of St. Faustina, the Holy Father quoted from her *Diary* and called the message she lived *the bridge to the third millennium*:

Jesus told Sr. Faustina: "*Humanity will not find peace until it turns trustfully to divine mercy*" [*Diary*, 300]. Through the work of the Polish religious, this message has become linked for ever to the 20th century, the last of the second millennium and the bridge to the third. It is not a new message but can be considered a gift of special enlightenment that helps us to relive the Gospel of Easter more intensely, to offer it as a ray of light to the men and women of our time. (April 30, 2000, n. 2, emphasis in original)

Then the Pope explained his intention of the canonization:

Sr. Faustina's canonization has a particular eloquence: by this act I intend today to pass this message on to the new millennium. I pass it on to all people. (Ibid., n. 5)

Three times Pope John Paul II repeated that the life and message of St. Faustina is *God's gift to our time.* He challenged us to welcome and receive God's mercy in order that we may be merciful to others: "The love of God and love of one's brothers and sisters are inseparable" (ibid., n. 5). He prayed that through the intercession of St. Faustina we may experience God's mercy and consolation as we sincerely profess, "Jesus, I trust in You!"

The Holy Father also "canonized" the Divine Mercy message and devotion, symbolized by the declaration of Divine Mercy Sunday:

It is important then that we accept the whole message that comes to us from the word of God on this Second Sunday of Easter, which from now on throughout the Church *will be called "Divine Mercy Sunday."* (April 30, 2000, n. 4, emphasis in original)

At the end of the Mass of Canonization, the Pope spoke in English, French, and Polish:

In the new millennium may the message of the merciful love of God, who bends over human poverty, be an endless source of hope for everyone and a call to show active love to one's brothers and sisters. (*Regina Caeli* talk [April 30, 2000])

At the end of the evening prayer service in St. Peter's Square the Holy Father exhorted us again:

I urge you always to trust in God's merciful love revealed to us in Christ Jesus, who died and rose again for our salvation.... Make Sr. Faustina's beautiful exclamation your own: Jesus, I trust in you! (April 30, 2000)

Chapter 7

Practical Ways to Live the Merciful Way

The following practical ways to live the merciful way are offered to you as ways that *work*. I know these work, not only from my own experience but from that of many holy men and women living today and those who have gone before us — especially St. Faustina.

Try them. You'll like them!

1. *Sacraments* (God's solemn oaths). Make frequent and regular use of the sacraments.

- *Holy Mass* — frequently and even daily if possible. "The most solemn moment of my life ..." (*Diary*, 1804).
- *Reconciliation (Confession)* — regularly, monthly, or even weekly. Not only are our sins forgiven in this sacrament, but we are also healed and taught and made more sensitive to the inspiration of the Holy Spirit (see *Diary*, 291 and 377). "**In the tribunal of mercy ... the greatest miracles take place**

[and] are incessantly repeated" (*Diary*, 1448).
- *Eucharistic Adoration:* During her working day, St. Faustina used every free moment to stop before the Blessed Sacrament and visit the Lord. She also spent special holy hours of adoration interceding for other people, especially those lost in sin.
- *Spiritual Communion* — If Holy Mass and the Blessed Sacrament are not available to you through the day, you can make repeated "spiritual communions." For a short moment (fifteen seconds to one minute), stop and turn to Jesus, who is present in your heart. "In your hearts reverence Christ as Lord" (1 Pt 3:15). Be present with your heart to the One who is present! No words are necessary — only love, thanksgiving, and adoration.

2. *Prayer Time.*

- Take time each day. Take time in your prayer corner to be with the Lord.
- Take time for *silent* presence to the Lord.
- Take time for your favorite devotional prayers.
- Take time for reading Sacred Scripture, especially the Gospels and Epistles.

- Take time for offering and entrusting your pains, your intentions, and your concerns to the Lord.

3. ***"Jubilate" with Jesus in the Holy Spirit*** (see Lk 10:21).

- When Jesus rejoiced in the Holy Spirit, He thanked and adored the Father, He "jubilated," He sang psalms: "And when they had sung a hymn, they went out to the Mount of Olives" (Mt 26:30), singing the traditional Hallel (Psalms 114-118).
- Like David, Jesus would have jubilated (see Lk 10:21) by dancing in praise of the Father.
- We, too, can jubilate in the Holy Spirit and dance and sing with Jesus to the glory of God the Father.
- The way to the Father's house is a three-step dance with Jesus, following the three steps of Jesus' death, resurrection, and reigning.
- We, too, can dance with Jesus as we die to self, rise by the Spirit, and reign with Him.
- In our times of misery and tribulation (see Rev 1:9), dance the three steps of the merciful way with Jesus:

    1. I *Trust* in Jesus (or *Entrust* to Jesus).

2. I *Rejoice* in the Holy Spirit.
3. I give *Thanks* to the Father with Jesus in the Holy Spirit.

- I *Trust (Entrust)* / I *Rejoice* / I *Thank* are repeated over and over as we are led by Jesus, higher and higher, to the house of the Father (see Jn 14:1-2).
- Trust and Thanks: "T 'n' T" is an explosive combination. It's dynamite! You will "exalt with all your heart" (Zeph 3:14). You will jubilate!

4. *Live the ABC's of Mercy.*

Ask for His mercy.
Be merciful.
Completely trust in Jesus!

5. *Glorify the mercy of God in and with the Heart of Jesus.*

6. *Pray unceasingly: JESUS, I TRUST IN YOU!*

To pray St. Faustina's exclamation of trust is to pray without ceasing our "yes," our *fiat*, with Mary, Mother of Mercy. It is to express our faith, hope, and love of the Father, the Son, and the Holy Spirit. It is to express our abandonment "to the truth of the word of the living God, knowing and humbly recognizing 'how unsearchable are his judgments and how inscrutable his ways' (Rom 11:33)" (Pope John Paul II, *Mother of the Redeemer* [1987], n. 14).

7. ***Tell others of the merciful way*** (and evangelize by praying and even singing).

- *Turn* to mercy now with ever greater *trust*, and you'll find joy, joy, joy.
- *Receive* His mercy now with ever greater *thanks,* and you'll find joy, joy, joy.
- *Share* His mercy now with ever greater *love,* and you'll find joy, joy, joy.

This is a way to live the *Magnificat* of Mary!

8. ***Live the merciful way.***

- It is the way for the third millennium.
- It is God's gift for our time.

Ask about all the books in the
Pocket Guide series!

A Pocket Guide to Confession
By Michael Dubruiel
978-1-59276-331-4 (ID# T430)

A Pocket Guide to the Mass
By Michael Dubruiel
978-1-59276-293-4 (ID# T383)

A Pocket Guide to the Meaning of Life
By Peter Kreeft
978-1-59276-300-9 (ID# T392)

A Pocket Guide to Purgatory
By Patrick Madrid
978-1-59276-294-1 (ID# T384)

OurSundayVisitor

Bringing Your Catholic Faith to Life
www.osv.com

A83BBBBP

1-800-348-2440 x3